©karla dornacher • karladornacher.com • facebook.com/karladornacher • karladornacher.etsy.com

This book belongs to

_____

_____

©karla dornacher • karladornacher.com • facebook.com/karladornacher • karladornacher.etsy.com

GARDEN BLESSINGS

Adult Coloring Book

Scriptures and Inspirations to Color Your World

Art & Design by Karla Dornacher

Copyright
Copyright ©2015 Karla Dornacher Designs. All rights reserved.
COPY PERMISSION - The illustrations in this book are designed for personal use only.
Permission is granted by author/artist to reproduce pages for coloring for small group gatherings
such as family gatherings, Bible study groups, Sunday School, etc.
Any other use, especially commercial use of selling of art - as is or colored -
is strictly prohibited in any form, including digitally or mechanically.
If you should choose to share a colored page on your blog or FB page,
please include a link back to my website or etsy shop so your friends can find me too. Thank you
For licinsing inquiries or other permissions contact karladornacher@gmail.com

karladornacher.com • karladornacher.etsy.com * facebook.com/karladornacher
Karla Dornacher Designs
Vancouver, WA 98664

I have always known my ability to draw was a gift and once I became aware that this gift was from God,
it has been my desire to use my art to glorify the Lord and be a blessing to others.
I am so grateful to be able to combine my two passions...
living creatively and encouraging others through God's Word...
as a way to share my heart with you through the delightful pages of this garden inspired coloring book.

Each of my illustrations was created with the hope that you would enjoy a quiet time to relax
and find rest for your soul... not only through the peaceful pleasure of creative coloring...
but even more importantly through time spent meditating and reflecting on God's Word...
allowing His truths to calm your heart and encourage your faith.

Remember... there is no right or wrong way to color!
It's all about enjoying the process... choosing your own color palette... unleashing your own inner artist!
My designs are perfect for crayons, colored pencils, watercolor pencils, markers, and gel pens.
You might want to try a light watercolor wash over an area and then fill in only a flower here and there.
When using colored pencils you can add depth of color by layering darker tones over light ones.
To help prevent colors from bleeding through the back side of the page when using water or markers,
place a blank sheet of paper between the pages when coloring.

You will find the designs in this book are printed on the front of the pages only.
This will enable you to remove them from the book, trim on the thin border to 8"x10",
and drop into a standard size frame for gift giving or for your own pleasure and encouragement.

May God truly bless the creativity of your heart and hands...
and, in turn, use you to glorify Him and be a blessing to others!
With love and God-hugs...
Karla

Contents

Bible verses and inspiring words
to encourage your heart and lift your spirit!

©karla dornacher • karladornacher.com • facebook.com/karladornacher • karladornacher.etsy.com

welcome

Throughout the Bible... from the first pages to the last... we see God portrayed as the Master Gardener of the earth, our spiritual lives, and the garden of our hearts.

I have always been fascinated with the garden imagery of the scriptures. I love how God uses these word pictures to convey spiritual truths in ways we can visualize and more easily understand His will and ways.

So whether you are an avid gardener, a casual cultivator, or don't like to dig in the dirt at all... I believe we can all relate to and delight in the beauty and bounty of a well-tended garden...
especially one overflowing with fragrant flowers and singing birds!

So... I invite you to stroll with me through the pages of "Garden Blessings"... reflecting on God's Word as you add your own creative color and personal touch along the way.

Please... enjoy your time here. Sit quietly with the Lord. Let Him plant a few seeds in the garden of your heart... and may your roots grow a little deeper in His love as you do.

Your garden friend...

Karla

©karla dornacher • karladornacher.com • facebook.com/karladornacher • karladornacher.etsy.com

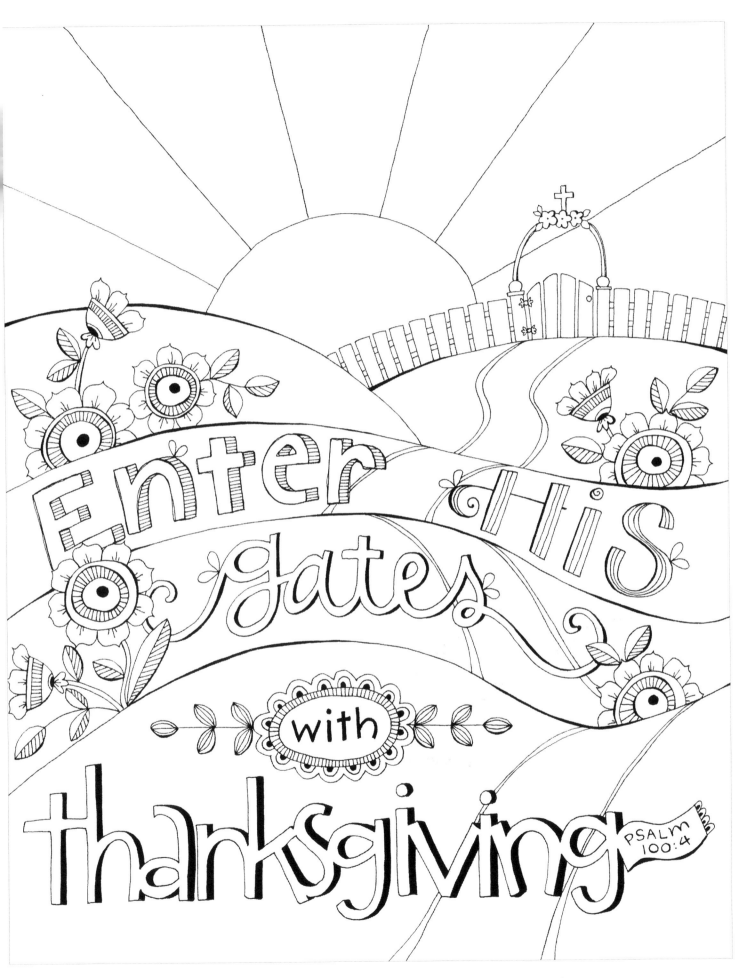

Enter His gates with thanksgiving PSALM 100:4

©karla dornacher • karladornacher.com • facebook.com/karladornacher • karladornacher.etsy.com

Forget not all
His benefits

Forget-Me-Not

seeds of praise
PSALM 103:2

©karla dornacher • karladornacher.com • facebook.com/karladornacher • karladornacher.etsy.com

May your Roots go down deep
into the soil of God's marvelous love...

↬ EPHESIANS 3:17 ↫

©karla dornacher • karladornacher.com • facebook.com/karladornacher • karladornacher.etsy.com

©karla dornacher • karladornacher.com • facebook.com/karladornacher • karladornacher.etsy.com

Be still and know that I am God

PSALM 46:10

©karla dornacher • karladornacher.com • facebook.com/karladornacher • karladornacher.etsy.com

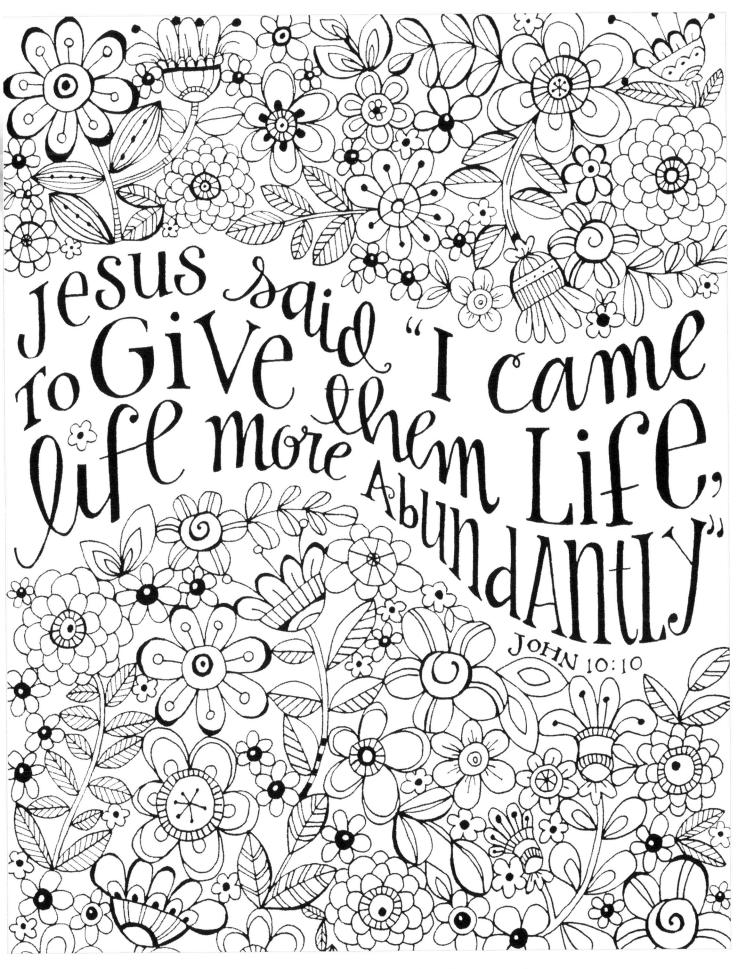

Jesus said to Give them Life, "I came to Give life more Abundantly" JOHN 10:10

©karla dornacher • karladornacher.com • facebook.com/karladornacher • karladornacher.etsy.com

your SOUL shall be like a well~watered Garden

Isaiah 58:11

©karla dornacher • karladornacher.com • facebook.com/karladornacher • karladornacher.etsy.com

©karla dornacher • karladornacher.com • facebook.com/karladornacher • karladornacher.etsy.com

We (are) to God the fragrance of Christ

2 Corinthians 2:15

©karla dornacher • karladornacher.com • facebook.com/karladornacher • karladornacher.etsy.com

above ALL put on love

Colossians 3:14

©karla dornacher • karladornacher.com • facebook.com/karladornacher • karladornacher.etsy.com

A friend loves at all times

PROVERBS 17:17

©karla dornacher • karladornacher.com • facebook.com/karladornacher • karladornacher.etsy.com

Scatter seeds of blessing wherever you go.

©karla dornacher • karladornacher.com • facebook.com / karladornacher • karladornacher.etsy.com

so we being many are one body in Christ

many flowers... one bouquet

1 Corinthians 12:20

©karla dornacher • karladornacher.com • facebook.com/karladornacher • karladornacher.etsy.com

He LEADS me
beside Quiet WATERS

Psalm 23:2

©karla dornacher • karladornacher.com • facebook.com/karladornacher • karladornacher.etsy.com

He who SOWS bountifully will also REAP bountifully

1 Corinthians 9:6

©karla dornacher • karladornacher.com • facebook.com/karladornacher • karladornacher.etsy.com

hope

Be strong and take heart, all you who hope in the Lord.

PSALM 31:24

heavenly seeds of promise

©karla dornacher • karladornacher.com • facebook.com / karladornacher • karladornacher.etsy.com

every DAY brings new wonders to behold

©karla dornacher • karladornacher.com • facebook.com/karladornacher • karladornacher.etsy.com

Search my heart, O God

from Psalm 139:23

©karla dornacher • karladornacher.com • facebook.com/karladornacher • karladornacher.etsy.com

to everything there is a season

Ecclesiastes 3:1

©karla dornacher • karladornacher.com • facebook.com/karladornacher • karladornacher.etsy.com

PLANT God's Word in your heart. **WATER** it with plenty of prayer. **FERTILIZE** it with faith and obedience. **Harvest** the **blessings** with **praise** and thanksgiving!

©karla dornacher • karladornacher.com • facebook.com/karladornacher • karladornacher.etsy.com

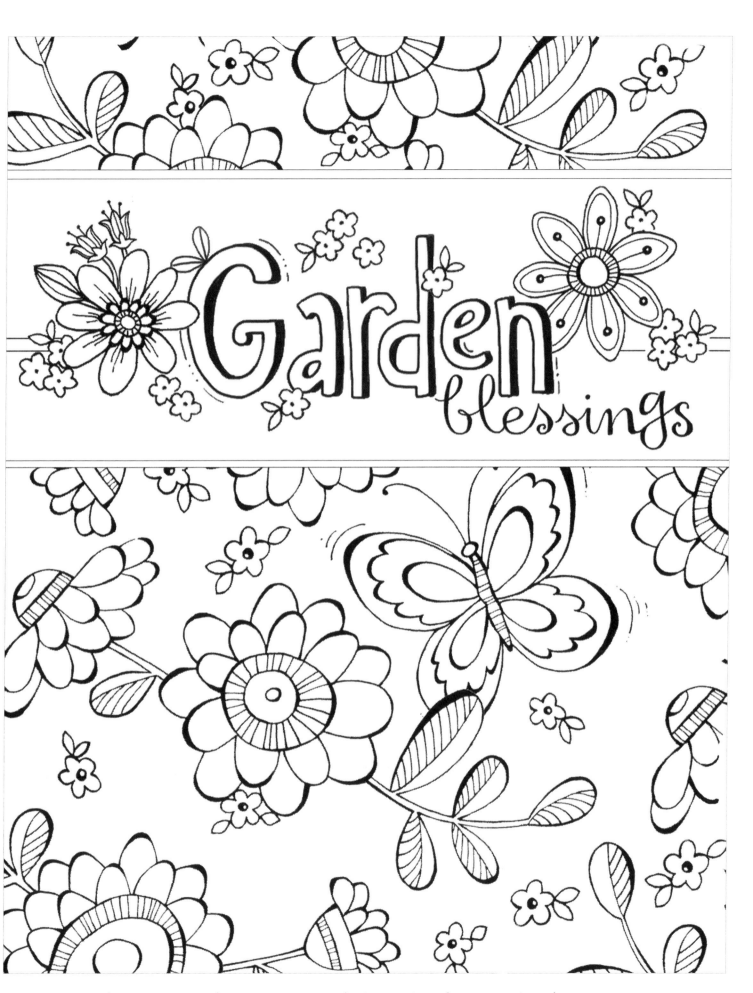

Garden blessings

©karla dornacher • karladornacher.com • facebook.com/karladornacher • karladornacher.etsy.com

This is the **DAY** that the **Lord** has made we will **rejoice** and **BE glad** in it. Psalm 118:24

Oh **Sing** to the **Lord** a new **Song** Psalm 98:1

If **anyone** is in **Christ** he is a **new creation** 1 Corinthians 5:17

Let the **whole earth** be filled with **its GLORY** Psalm 72:19

Copy, Color and Cut!
Perfect size to fit in the margin of your Journaling Bible...
or make as many copies as you need for gift giving or ministry use!

©karla dornacher • karladornacher.com • facebook.com/karladornacher • karladornacher.etsy.com

Words of Blessing Bookmarks

CHOOSE joy

faith

is not hoping God can... but knowing He will.

LOVE never fails

hope ALWAYS

Color and Cut!
Use for Bible Journaling, scrapbooking or any and all paper crafting.
Print as many copies as you need for personal use, gift giving or ministry use!

©karla dornacher • karladornacher.com • facebook.com/karladornacher • karladornacher.etsy.com

Thank you again for buying my Garden Blessings Coloring Book.
I hope you have delighted in some special moments with God,
the Master Gardener of your heart.
I pray you've found a little rest for your soul in His Word nestled amongst
the blossoms, birds and butterflies along the way.
And I hope you've been inspired and encouraged to be creative and clever
in your own personal expression of color and play.

For more inspiration, free downloads, and current news and updates visit:
www.karladornacher.com
www.karladornacher.typepad.com
www.facebook.com/karladornacher

To shop for more "Color Your Own" digital art including Bible bookmarks and
Blessing Cards... as well as my fine art prints... please visit:
www.karladornacher.etsy.com

God bless you and keep you...
in His love... and always for His glory...
Karla

©karla dornacher • karladornacher.com • facebook.com/karladornacher • karladornacher.etsy.com

48077321R00035

Made in the USA
Lexington, KY
19 December 2015